BEETHOVEN

EASIER PIANO VARIATIONS

Edited and Recorded by Immanuela Gruenberg

AUDIO ACCESS INCLUDED
Recorded Performances Online

To access companion recorded performances online, visit:
www.halleonard.com/mylibrary

Enter Code
2233-5913-0714-7677

On the cover:
Northern Landscape (1822)
by Johan Christian Dahl (1788–1857)

ISBN 978-1-4584-1924-8

G. SCHIRMER, *Inc.*

DISTRIBUTED BY

7777 W. BLUEMOUND RD. P.O. BOX 13819 MILWAUKEE, WI 53213

www.musicsalesclassical.com
www.halleonard.com

CONTENTS

The price of this publication includes access to companion recorded performances online, for download or streaming, using the unique code found on the title page. Visit **www.halleonard.com/mylibrary** and enter the access code.

LISTING OF INDIVIDUAL VARIATIONS

PAGE		LOCATION WITHIN AUDIO TRACK
	Six Variations on a Swiss Song, WoO 64	
14	Theme	0:00
14	Variation I	0:32
15	Variation II	0:58
15	Variation III	1:25
16	Variation IV	2:16
16	Variation V	2:35
17	Variation VI	2:59
17	Coda	3:18
	Nine Variations on "Quant' è più bello" from *La Molinara* by Giovanni Paisiello, WoO 69	
18	Theme	0:00
19	Variation I	0:34
20	Variation II	1:02
21	Variation III	1:32
22	Variation IV	2:04
23	Variation V	2:49
24	Variation VI	3:22
25	Variation VII	3:48
26	Variation VIII	4:17
27	Variation IX	4:45
	Six Variations on "Nel cor più non mi sento" from *La Molinara* by Giovanni Paisiello, WoO 70	
30	Theme	0:00
30	Variation I	0:54
32	Variation II	1:43
33	Variation III	2:28
34	Variation IV	3:15
34	Variation V	4:24
36	Variation VI	5:08
	Eight Variations on "Une fièvre brûlante" from *Richard Coeur de Lion* by André Ernest Modeste Grétry, WoO 72	
38	Theme	0:00
38	Variation I	0:58
40	Variation II	1:48
41	Variation III	2:35
43	Variation IV	3:21
44	Variation V	4:26
45	Variation VI	5:15
46	Variation VII	6:00
48	Variation VIII	6:51
50	Coda	7:47
	Six Easy Variations in G Major, WoO 77	
52	Theme	0:00
52	Variation I	1:14
53	Variation II	2:18
54	Variation III	3:16
55	Variation IV	4:11
56	Variation V	5:56
57	Variation VI	6:55
59	Coda	7:54

The times cited are for the beginning of a variation within the track.

HISTORICAL NOTES

Ludwig van Beethoven (1770–1827)

The nearly mythical figure of Beethoven looms as large today as it did in his own century. No one has dominated his own musical milieu in quite the same way as Beethoven; no one has inspired and intimidated as many composers for as long a period as Beethoven; and certainly no other composer accomplished all of this while lacking his hearing, unarguably a musician's most important sense.

Beethoven realized he was becoming deaf in his early 30s after years of prominence in the Viennese music scene. He had moved to Vienna from his hometown of Bonn in 1792 at the age of 22. Initially he studied composition with Joseph Haydn and other distinguished composers. Three years after his arrival, he carefully orchestrated his public debut by timing the publication of his first several opus numbers with the premiere performance of a piano concerto (likely Concerto No. 1, the second one he had in fact written). The success of this initial flurry established Beethoven as an extraordinary musical presence virtually from the outset, and he remained an honored, albeit eccentric, celebrity in Vienna for the rest of his life.

Although born into a modest family of musicians, Beethoven moved in aristocratic circles by virtue of his genius. Members of the Viennese nobility comprised some of the more musically sophisticated patrons in all of Europe, and they commissioned dozens of works from Beethoven. For these commissions, the patron would specify the genre and the difficulty for each piece, and Beethoven could be as creative as he desired within the technical parameters. The two parties agreed on a period of time (six months, or a year, say) when the patron had exclusive rights to perform but not circulate the work, after which Beethoven was free to publish it. Beethoven prospered from these commissions and subsequent publications, living essentially without financial worry until his death in 1827.

For any great artist, music is not merely a means of feeding oneself, though such necessities are too easily discounted when we consider a life 200 years later. Acutely aware of his ambition for artistic greatness, Beethoven needed to convince publishers to rally behind his more difficult works in order to fulfill his artistic destiny. When Beethoven published a work he considered musically significant, he would assign an opus number to it. On more than one occasion, such works might have lacked immediate public appeal and money-making potential, so Beethoven would often induce publishers to produce these pieces by promising additional, less challenging works to be published without an opus number (abbreviated WoO in German). Sometimes Beethoven offered several works—both with and without an opus—as a package deal to a publisher.

Once a piece was ready for publication, Beethoven (or his representative) negotiated a contract that often involved a single fee for the work. The payment of royalties—additional money based on the number of copies sold—did not enter into the transaction, in part because the work would likely be pirated by a rival publisher within a couple of weeks. Given the financial risks of piracy, Beethoven wisely provided incentives, through his WoO works, to print the more daring works for which profits would have been less assured.

Of the two distinct categories of Beethoven's output—those with opus numbers and those without—this volume draws from the latter. In many cases, the pieces in the WoO category present an excellent introduction to performing Beethoven, particularly since most listeners know of Beethoven's greatness first and foremost through his more famous, numbered works.

–Denise Pilmer Taylor

PERFORMANCE NOTES

Why Study Variations?

Variations are wonderful for teaching and for performing. Variation sets consist of small parts, each with its own technical and musical idiosyncrasies and challenges. The compact size and the specific characteristics of each variation make them much easier to learn than sonata or even sonatina movements which are usually longer and contain an assortment of challenges in each movement. Because students can learn each variation faster than they would a sonata or sonatina movement, there is less of a risk they will grow tired, bored, or frustrated with the piece before they have reached a satisfactory performance level. By examining each variation's character and makeup, students learn about themes and their possible expansion, motives and motivic development, harmonic progressions, and so on. An additional perk is that once a student has mastered all the variations in a set, it is very satisfying to be able to perform all of them as elements that make up a single, larger composition.

Beethoven and the Variation

One of the main characteristics of Beethoven's compositional style was his ability to take a musical idea and break it into its smallest motives, and then use these motives as building blocks, altering and presenting them in new ways. Beethoven employed this creative style throughout his entire life and entire oeuvre. It is not surprising that variations—a musical form that is based on presenting musical ideas in different ways and in a variety of guises and alterations—played an important role in Beethoven's musical output throughout his career.

In his early variations, Beethoven employs many elements of Viennese music at the time, and specifically of Viennese variations, including clear texture, figurations, a minor-mode variation in a major-key set, variations based on one of various rhythmic values or patterns (eighth notes, sixteenths, dotted rhythms, or triplets) to modify and disguise the theme or its motives. These elements can all be found in many of Mozart's variations as far back as K. 25, which Mozart composed when he was ten years old.

Beethoven composed a total of twenty sets of variations during his lifetime. His first set of variations was published when he was only eleven years old and his last set, the Diabelli Variations, Op. 120, he composed at age fifty-three. The present volume contains five of the twelve sets written over a ten-year period from 1790 to 1800. The variations appear here in chronological order, allowing the performer to easily track changes in Beethoven's compositional style, even within a relatively short period of time.

The first set in this volume, WoO 64, was composed in 1790 while Beethoven was still in Bonn. Beethoven arrived in Vienna in November 1792 and studied with Haydn for about a year. Haydn, upon his departure for London in January 1794, passed Beethoven on to Johann Georg Albrechtsberger, Vienna's best known teacher of counterpoint. [1]

The following two sets, WoO 69 and 70, were completed in 1795. Beethoven's output of piano works in 1795 included the Piano Concerto No. 1 in C Major, Op. 15, the three piano trios of opus 1, the first three piano sonatas opus 2, and various smaller works, including "Rage Over a Lost Penny" as well as four sets of piano variations, two of which are included in this edition.

In these five sets, the basic tempo of the themes and of most variations is moderate, ranging from *Andante con moto* to *Andante quasi Allegretto* and *Allegretto.* Of the five themes and 35 variations, one variation is marked *Allegro* and one is marked *Tempo di Menuetto* (number VIII from WoO 72 in C Major and number IX from WoO 69 in A Major, respectively). It is interesting to note the mostly restrained character of these variations—no extreme tempos or dynamics and no unexpected harmonies—and their generally transparent textures. This restraint is present despite the fact that Beethoven had concurrently composed various large-scale works with wide dynamic ranges, varied tempos and moods, and remarkable textures. See discussion of each set.

Beethoven and the Piano

Between 1790 and 1800, the period during which these variations were composed, Beethoven had at his disposal several Viennese fortepianos: a Stein—which, like Mozart, he seemed to prefer—and apparently also a Walter, and a Späth. The typical range was five octaves, FF–f'''. The tone was softer, had less of a singing quality, and decayed faster than on the modern piano. In a letter to Streicher, the famous piano maker, Beethoven complains that when one listens to the fortepiano, "one often thinks that one is merely listening to the harp." [2] Beethoven further claims that Streicher was "one of the few who realize[d] and perceive[d] that, provided one can feel the music, one can also make the pianoforte sing. I hope that the time will come when the harp and the pianoforte will be treated as two entirely different instruments." [3]

The fortepiano was undergoing many changes during Beethoven's lifetime. One of these changes was the expanding range from five to five-and-a-half and then six octaves. In his music, Beethoven pushed the limits of the instruments just as he struggled against the boundaries of form. His lifelong association with Streicher helped bring about changes to the pianoforte, which Beethoven wished for and Streicher incorporated.

Reports from his contemporaries and acquaintances give us some ideas about how he himself played. Beethoven "played with great technical facility [...] he excelled in legato playing; and he commanded special attention for the depth of his expressive playing, particularly in slow movements." [4]

Style and Interpretation

Only few performance indications, such as tempo or dynamics, are present in these works. In general Beethoven used a greater number and a larger variety of markings in his later works. In his excellent book, *Beethoven on Beethoven: Playing His Music His Way*, William S. Newman writes that "Beethoven ordinarily waited until his sketches had been converted into or replaced by final autographs—that is, until the notation was completed—before inserting articulation, expression, and other performance markings." [5]

The manuscript of the Swiss Song variations, WoO 64, an unusually clean copy by Beethoven's standards, is the only known manuscript that survives of the five works in this edition. Even this manuscript, apparently prepared by Beethoven for the engravers, has very few performance indications. The lack of more precise, detailed instructions requires that performers be well-versed in the style of the young Beethoven so that any guesses they are compelled to make are educated guesses and are combined with fine artistic taste and good judgment.

Dynamics

These works contain relatively few dynamic markings. For a more thorough examination of this topic, see the discussion of each work.

Accents

Beethoven used a number of different symbols to indicate different kinds of accents. These works contain a large number of accents, mostly *sforzando* (***sf***) indications, often syncopated. This practice, evident already in his early works, turned into a convention of Beethoven's: "In Beethoven's sonatas [...] ***f*** accounts for only 10 percent and ***p*** for 18 percent of dynamics, while ***sf*** takes 30 percent ..." [6] "[...] ***sf*** is the most frequently used accent indication in the music of Beethoven. It appears in every dynamic context and is interpreted accordingly. He used the stroke and ***f*** less frequently, the latter occasionally replacing ***sf*** in a forte setting. [...]" [7] "In Beethoven's music the accent sign has its own role: it occurs almost always in *piano* or *pianissimo* settings and often on syncopated notes. [...] Clearly, for Beethoven ***sf*** was the stronger accent." [8]

Accentuation can be done through volume, by playing the accented note(s) louder, or through the use of timing—agogic accents—by lingering on or before the note just an instant longer than its rhythmic value indicates.

Sforzando (***sf***) appears in four (WoO 69, 70, 72 and 77) out of the five sets in this edition. A ***sf*** on strong beats (WoO 69, variation I, mm. 29–30) denotes added emphasis on a note that is naturally strong because of its metric accent. A ***sf*** on a weak beat (variation I, mm. 41 and 43) and the weak part of a strong or a weak beat (variation II, mm. 61 and 69 and WoO 70, variation I, mm. 25, 26, 35, etc.) can be expressive, playful, or unexpected—against the natural metric feel.

The wedge, which denotes an accented staccato, appears in the theme of WoO 64.

Rinforzando (*rinf.*) indicates a sudden, unprepared louder note or short crescendo over a few notes but it is less extreme than ***sf***. In WoO 69, variation IV, mm. 105, 107, 113, and 115, the *rinf.* indicates that these octaves should be slightly louder than the surrounding ones.

Touch

The basic, default touch during the early Classic period was *non legato*. When composers desired for a different touch, such as *legato* or *staccato*, they usually indicated it. Still, one should remember that Beethoven loved a *legato*, singing tone, a tone that was hard to achieve on Viennese fortepianos (see Beethoven and the Piano, above).

A variety of touches and articulations are found in these variations.

Portato, indicated by a slur over notes with dots refers to detached, slightly shorter notes than the basic *non-legato* ones but longer than *staccato*. *Staccato* is shorter than *portato* and is noted by dots over or under the notes. Wedges or strokes are wedge-shaped signs or short lines over the notes that indicate notes are played shorter than *staccato* and often also denote a slight accent.

That said, it is important to note a long-standing problem concerning these symbols. Beethoven's manuscripts often make it hard, and sometimes even impossible, to distinguish between dots and strokes or wedges. This can be seen on the Beethoven-Haus Bonn website: http://www.beethoven-haus-bonn.de/sixcms/detail.php?template=dokseite_digitales_archiv_en&_dokid=wm254&suchparameter=dokartx:x:x12x-x-xpersonx:x:xBeethoven,%20Ludwig%20van&_sucheinstieg=handschriftensuche&_seite=1-4

In the above example the markings often look as if they could be either *portato* or *staccato*. To make matters worse, sometimes when such signs do appear visually unambiguous, they do not necessarily make musical sense and at times they seem inconsistent. This issue applies only to WoO 64 as it is the only set for which a manuscript exists. Since no manuscripts for the other sets are known to be extant, we rely on early editions, and therefore encounter no issues related to unintelligible handwriting.

Like dynamics, tempo, and all other aspects involved in interpreting and executing a musical composition, musical signs and indications have to be interpreted in context. *Staccato* notes in a loud passage may be shorter than similar notes in a *piano* passage even if the tempo is the same. Likewise, different tempos will affect the touch, articulation, and dynamics.

Period pianos did not allow for *legato* as we've come to know it on the modern piano, with its sustained, slow-decaying sound (see Beethoven's complaint about the pianoforte, above). Evidence seems to point to Beethoven's desire for a *legato* sound and to the fact that he himself had a beautiful *legato*. Although this *legato* was obviously different from our modern-day one, performers should not shy away from *legato* where the music calls for it.

Tempo

The tempo indications of the five themes are as follows: *Andante con moto*, [*Andantino*], *Andante quasi allegretto*, and *Allegretto*—all moderate speeds. My own choice of tempos can be heard on the accompanying recordings, but it is important to note that, as with any performance, these are not written in stone; rather, they reflect my choices at a particular time.

Classic period tempos did not fluctuate within any one movement. Most movements had one basic, underlying tempo. Only minor modifications were considered acceptable, and these had to be carried out in a manner that made these modifications imperceptible. These variations also have an underlying tempo each, with only few exceptions indicated by Beethoven's tempo markings.

Trills and Ornaments

Among the various treatises written about early-classic performance practice, there is no real consensus regarding the execution of ornaments. Their realization and performance depend on the musical context: their place in the musical line, the notes that precede and follow them, tempo, harmony, the mood of the music, and so on. Ornaments, by nature, do not follow rigid rules. Probably the single most important "rule" to bear in mind in this regard is that the style and character of the ornaments should match the composer's intentions and the work's style and character.

Long trills were often used not only as ornaments, but also as a means to extend the sound of a note that would decay even faster on that period's piano than it does on the modern piano. Measures 164–165 and 188–189 in variation V of WoO 72 may be examples of such a case.

Grace notes were undergoing changes during the second half of the 18th century. Historical accounts tell us that among performers of the time there were those who adhered to the traditional way of interpreting grace notes—namely, playing them on the beat, taking their time from the note they preceded—while others were playing them before the beat, taking time from the note that preceded them. Quite a few treatises of the time chastise the latter. This criticism nevertheless points to a practice that was common enough at the time.

The realization of small notes often depends on the tempo of the piece. In a fast tempo these could be realized as grace notes (short and before the beat) while in a slow tempo, as appoggiaturas (longer and on the beat). "In a very general way we can view this moving of some small single notes to a pre-beat position as another step in the progression from the largely on-beat (and some afternote) performance in the late Baroque keyboard music to some very short on-beat ornaments, to anticipation in limited circumstances, and finally to the anticipation of all small single notes during the Romantic period."[9]

WoO
This stands for *Werke ohne Opuszahl* or Works without opus number, as per Georg Kinsky's Thematic Catalogue.

Comments on This Edition

Sources

The variations in F Major, WoO 64 are the only ones in this volume with known extant manuscript. Thanks to the excellent archive of the Beethoven-Haus Bonn, which is available online, consulting many invaluable original and early editions is as easy as a click on a link. In addition, I have also consulted the following editions: G. Henle, edited by Joseph Schmidt-Görg; Wiener Urtext Edition, edited by Erwin Ratz; G. Schirmer, edited by Hans von Bülow and Sigmund Lebert; C. F. Peters, edited by Peter Hauschild; and Breitkopf & Härtel's 1862–1890 Complete Edition of Beethoven's works.

Fingering

I have included fingerings only occasionally, mainly where I find a certain fingering particularly helpful or where I prefer what may seem to be unintuitive or non-standard fingering. These are, of course, only suggestions, as each hand is different. Students who learn these works at a young age may—and should—revisit their choice of fingering when relearning the pieces at an older age when their hands have changed and have become bigger. Beethoven's original fingerings, found in the manuscript and the first edition of WoO 64 are printed in italics.

Level of Difficulty

The variations appear in chronological order in this edition. Taking into account that students' strengths and limitations differ, a general guideline of easier to more difficult would be:

F Major, WoO 64
G Major, WoO 70
A Major, WoO 69
G Major, WoO 77
C Major, WoO 72

Accommodating Small Hands

Many of us, me included, have to sometimes roll chords that others can easily play blocked, simply because our hands aren't big enough. This is an acceptable practice. Some accommodations, such as leaving out notes from large chords or octaves, are unacceptable for adult pianists. However, I may occasionally suggest them as a temporary solution for younger students whose hands are still too small. I believe that if a student is otherwise capable of playing a certain composition, accommodations should be made for the student's small hands. Some such suggestions are included in the score.

Notes on the Individual Variations

Six Variations on a Swiss Song, WoO 64

Composed 1790

See discussion of the manuscript under Style and Interpretation above.

According to most sources the Six Variations on a Swiss Song were composed in 1790 while Beethoven was still in Bonn and before he left for Vienna to study with Haydn. This is Beethoven's second set of variations. He composed the first set, Nine Variations on a March by Dressler, WoO 63, at age eleven or twelve.

While pretty straightforward and not too advanced, this set is replete with technical and musical issues for students to tackle. These include a variety of touches: *legato, portato, staccato,* wedges, and melody and accompaniment played by the same hand; different and contrasting moods; a wide range of dynamics (from ***p*** to ***ff***); various rhythms; polyphony (mainly in variation V but also, to some extent, in the theme and in variations I, II and III); numerous technical issues. In addition to the variety of touches mentioned above, other challenges include octaves, runs, and double thirds.

The 11-measure-long theme is different from the more standard 8- or 16-measure themes. The opening, or question part, is 6 measures long; the closing, or answer, is 5 measures. The theme's melodic contour is easily identifiable through all six variations.

Beethoven meticulously marks the various touches intended for the theme: *portato* for the quarter notes, wedges for the half notes. In spite of the theme being *detaché* throughout, it should flow smoothly and with a sense of continuity.

Variations I and II have no execution indications whatsoever: neither of dynamics, nor of mood or character, nor of touch. The uninterrupted flow of triplets between the two hands makes it easy to achieve a sense of continuity in variation I. By contrast, variation II is marked by the angularity of the dotted rhythm. The performer has to be careful to maintain the melodic character of the theme played by the right hand against the left-hand's dotted rhythm.

Dynamic indications first appear in variation III: *sempre piano e legato*. In a minor mode, this variation should be clearly voiced and played *legato* throughout.

An artistic challenge is presented by the dialogue of the two independent lines in variation VI. Though not the most technically difficult, variation VI is the most complex of the set. Sudden dynamic shifts (between ***ff*** and ***p***), octaves, fast scale and arpeggio runs, and trills drive this set, which starts out quietly and simply, toward what seems like a brilliant finale, only to suddenly scale back and end quietly and innocently.

Nine Variations on "Quant' è più bello" from *La Molinara* by Giovanni Paisiello, WoO 69

Composed 1795

Composed in 1788, Paisiello's comic opera *La Molinara* enjoyed great success and popularity over a period of four decades. A number of different arrangements were made based on its music, and several composers besides Beethoven wrote variations based on its arias. "Quant' è più bello," was incorporated into this opera but was not written by Paisiello himself.

A few things to bear in mind regarding this piece and its performance.

- With only one exception—the last note of variation II—Beethoven stays away from the keyboard's very low register. He occasionally uses the piano's high register, but for the most part he stays within the middle range. This is significant given the fact that on Beethoven's piano the different registers had different tone colors. By staying (mostly) within one range, Beethoven stayed (mostly) within the same timbre.
- From the theme and through variation III there is a slight but consistent increase in velocity (over a steady beat). The theme is marked by eighth notes, variation I consists of triplets, followed by variation II which is marked by sixteenths, and variation III incorporates sextuplets. This increase in the speed of notes gives a sense of forward motion and continuity from one variation to the next, an important feature in a form that, if not properly structured and performed, may come off as disjointed. To achieve this sense of forward motion it is important that the performer not slow down.
- Variation IV is lyrical. *Legato* octaves can be challenging, especially for those with smaller hands. A suggestion for redistributing the notes between the hands is included in the score.
- Variation V is the first one in this set marked ***pp***.
- The indication *rinforzando* (*rinf.*), present only in variation VI, is a short *crescendo* or an expressive emphasis less extreme than *sforzando*, the accent prevalent in all the other variations.
- Variation IX concludes the set in a *Tempo di Menuetto*, in triple meter, in contrast with the duple meter of the theme and all preceding variations. Its dynamic range, from *pianissimo* to *fortissimo*, is wide. Additionally, it is the only variation in the set that breaks away from the theme's simple harmonic language by using modulation (to the relative key of F-sharp minor).

Six Variations on "Nel cor più non mi sento" from *La Molinara* by Giovanni Paisiello, WoO 70

Composed 1795

Composed the same year as the "Quant' è più bello" variations, these too are based on an aria from Paisiello's *La Molinara*. See above for the significance of 1795 in Beethoven's output for the piano and for a brief discussion of *La Molinara*.

"Nel cor più non mi sento" was probably the most popular of the opera's many successful arias. Johann Nepomuk Hummel and Niccolò Paganini are among the many composers who composed variations on this lovely aria.

As instrumentalists, we regularly sing in order to better feel the shape and emotion of a musical line. For an instrumental work that is based on an aria, nothing is more natural, more helpful, or more instructive than beginning at the source. Listen to the aria performed by a singer. The great number of performances available of this aria are proof of its continued popularity.

The beautiful lyrical theme in a gently flowing 6/8 time sets the stage for a composition that is lovely throughout. The theme's entire melodic line is present in all six variations. The beauty and charm of this set should not obscure the wide range of emotions, moods, and pianistic characteristics incorporated into these variations.

One challenge performers face is this piece's near lack of execution markings. Dynamic markings appear in only one instance: measures 93–94 of variation IV. The only other performance markings are the many ***sf*** signs and the *staccatos* in the left hand of variation V. There are no tempo headings (not even for the theme) and there are only occasional slurs.

Figurations are introduced for the right hand in variation I with the left hand accompanying. This layout is reversed in variation II. The pianist should pay special attention to the off-beat, syncopated *sforzandos* in variation I. Whether interpreted as dynamic or agogic accents, they are in danger of sounding repetitive. They should instead have a cumulative effect, moving the line forward.

At first glance, the broken chords of variation III appear to correspond to only the harmonic progression of the theme; however, the melody is present in the broken chords' highest notes. These, therefore, should be played with a singing tone and a carefully shaped line.

In the expressive and lyrical variation IV, the performer should pay special attention to the off-beat two-note slurs in mm. 83, 85–87, 90, and 97–99. The first note in a two-note slur is somewhat louder than the second one. Their appearance in succession intensifies their expressiveness. Their being syncopated makes them all the more powerful.

This variation presents an opportunity for such *legato* expressive playing as discussed above in the section Beethoven and the Piano. It is nevertheless essential to remain faithful to late 18th-century style and not go overboard with personal expression.

Eight Variations on "Une fièvre brûlante" from *Richard Coeur de Lion* by André Ernest Modeste Grétry, WoO 72
Composed 1796

Among the other works that Beethoven composed in 1796 are the three piano sonatas of opus 10. The theme Beethoven used for these variations is a love song from the French Romantic comedy *Richard Coeur de Lion*. The variations begin with few performance instructions. Over the course of the eight variations the instructions grow in number, increase in details, the expressive range widens and the dynamic range expands to ***pp*** through ***ff***.

Performance instructions are nearly absent at the beginning of the variations. Aside from the *Allegretto* heading, Beethoven provides no performance indications whatsoever for the theme. Still, we do know it is based on an aria—a love song, to be exact—so it follows quite naturally that this theme should be played *cantabile* and with feeling.

Similar to his choices in WoO 69, Beethoven uses increasingly faster notes from the theme (quarter and half notes) through variation I (eighth notes), variation II (triplets), and variation III (sixteenths), before slowing down in variation IV, the one in the minor mode.

The 18th-century pianoforte did not have as uniform a sound across the keyboard as the modern piano. Each register had a distinct color, timbre, and character. So when Beethoven uses the entire range of the keyboard, from FF#, the second-lowest note on his piano, to f‴ the highest, he also uses very different tone colors. Variation V, for example, makes extensive use of the high and more brilliant register of the piano. The right hand, with its various trills, shines over the melodic left hand.

Variation VI oscillates between several opposites: *forte* or *fortissimo* vs. *piano*, high vs. low registers, chords vs. single-note lines, and a sharp, dotted rhythm vs. lightly flowing, graceful lines. These contrasts, so characteristic of Beethoven's more mature style, should be clearly pronounced.

It is more difficult than it initially appears to perform variation VII beautifully. The main challenge lies in judiciously using the pedal to maintain the balance between the right-hand *legato* and left-hand *staccato*. If one chooses to keep the *staccato* clearly articulated, one has to use the pedal sparingly and use as much finger ***legato*** as possible along with careful voicing so as to bring out and sustain the melody. The *staccato* and *legato* should not interfere with each other.

The last variation is the only one with a tempo indication, *Allegro*. Lively and containing several brilliant passages, this variation is in duple time, in contrast with the triple meter of the theme and preceding variations. With a wide dynamic range of ***pp*** to ***ff*** and several *cresc.* markings, this vivacious variation also packs in drama—or wit, depending on one's viewpoint: an abrupt, mid-sentence cut on the dominant seventh which is followed by silence. The music continues to elude the much-anticipated tonic, resuming *pianissimo* in the lowered sub-mediant of A-flat (a deceptive cadence), before finally reaching the tonic in a *presto*, *forte* and *fortissimo* energetic ending.

Six Easy Variations in G Major, WoO 77
Composed 1800

This is the only one of the five sets written on an original theme. Indeed, this set of variations, the thirteenth Beethoven composed, is the first he ever wrote on an original theme. Interestingly, opus 34 in F Major, the next set of variations he would write, would also be on an original theme, and opus 35 in E-flat Major, the one after that, would be on a theme from his own Eroica Symphony.

Although the title claims these are Easy Variations, they are not the easiest in this collection, nor the easiest Beethoven had written at that time.

The theme and variations are in clear binary form. The theme is marked *piano*. It calls for a variety of touches and articulations: *legato, portato, staccato,* two-note slurs, and eighth-to-sixteenth slurs plus sixteenth rest, all clearly indicated in the score. The last of these rhythms also helps to emphasize the eighth notes of the ascending line, G, A, B in mm. 2–3.

At least on the surface, there appear to be a number of inconsistencies in this set of variations. For example, the articulation in the left hand of variation I is inconsistent with that of the theme. In the theme, the left hand slurs consistently connect three beats, or one-and-a-half measures: counts two-one-two as in the upbeat and m. 1, mm. 4–5 and 12–13:

or counts one-two-one, as in mm. 2–3, 6–7 and 14–15.

In variation I, the measures corresponding to the above measures are slurred differently (upbeat to downbeat) even though the notes are quite similar.

mm. (16)–18

mm. 20–23

mm. 28–29

These slurs are, however, consistent with the bass's back and forth motion between two octaves.

The other possible inconsistency occurs in variation VI and is discussed below.

Variation III, like the theme, has clearly detailed touch and articulation markings. *Tenuto* markings on every quarter note, the slurred eighth-to-sixteenth followed by a sixteenth rest, *staccato* on most other eighths, and slurs for most groups of four sixteenths. The performer must follow these detailed instructions without losing sight of the big picture. In measures 48–52, for example, the same rhythmic and melodic pattern repeats four times:

mm. (48)–52

In spite of the repetitiveness of this musical idea, all four measures should be executed as one continuous line that makes up the opening, antecedent, or "question" of the eight-measure phrase.

Variation VI is brilliant, with constant, seemingly relentless thirty-second notes. The absence of performance markings leaves room for various interpretations. I started out playing this variation on the brilliant side, *forte* and *non legato,* but later found a slightly less brilliant approach more to my liking. I think that this variation lends itself well to experimentation with quite different interpretations. I encourage performers to explore these.

This variation contains one noteworthy and rather intriguing musical puzzle, on which editors do not seem to agree. Measure 112b, namely, the second ending, is only one beat long. This one-beat measure results in a shift in the bar lines that, from this point to the Coda, seems to arrive one beat too early. This shift is especially noticeable upon the return to the variation's opening material in m. 117 which now occurs on the downbeat rather than the upbeat.

This is how the piece first appeared in print when published by Jean Traeg in 1800. Many subsequent editors, including those for modern editions like Joseph Schmidt-Görg (and Johannes Herzog) for G. Henle and Erwin Ratz for Universal/Wiener Urtext Edition have followed the first edition. Others, however, have attempted to correct (or "correct," depending on one's point of view) the potential oversight. Breitkopf & Härtel in their 1862–1890 Complete Edition of Beethoven's Works moved the bar lines starting at the second ending so that measure 112b is a full, two-beat measure:

mm. 110–112

This shifting of the bar lines places everything that follows in its "proper" place, consistent with the theme, the previous variations and the first half of this variation.

mm. 110–118, from *Ludwig van Beethoven's Werke: vollständige Kritisch durchgesehene überall berechtige Ausgable* (Breitkopt & Härtel, 1862–1888).

But this shift also shortens measure 120 where the Coda begins. To make up for this, Breitkopf & Härtel added a quarter note that extends the fermata into the next measure. The addition of this single beat makes no noticeable difference since it extends a fermata.

mm. 114–124, from *Ludwig van Beethoven's Werke: vollständige Kritisch durchgesehene überall berechtige Ausgable* (Breitkopt & Härtel, 1862–1888).

Sigmund Lebert and Hans von Bülow's 1898 edition for G. Schirmer, follows Breitkopf & Härtel.

Erwin Ratz, in his Critical Notes for the Wiener Urtext Edition, comments that Breitkopf & Härtel have made these changes

> [...] without a reason being given. There is no evidence to support such an alteration; neither can it be assumed that the OE [original edition] and all subsequent editions are wrong. Therefore, our text follows the OE despite the striking displacement, which Beethoven obviously intended.

The editors for Henle provide no comment on this phenomenon.

I have chosen the more widely accepted, unchanged version. This is primarily because the first edition appeared during Beethoven's lifetime; therefore, we can assume, though we can't be certain, that Beethoven had a chance to correct any obvious mistakes before publication. Of course, Beethoven may have missed this, but is it reasonable to just assume this? Did Beethoven intend to switch the up- and downbeats in these few measures of the last variation? How likely is it that he wanted to leave all other aspects of the piece—harmony, melody, phrase length—unchanged but to alter this?

What we have are many reliable sources, along with one version that contains some serious inconsistencies and a one-beat measure and another, "corrected," consistent edition. In our eagerness to be loyal to the sources—the older the source, the better—we try to avoid the latter. I draw attention to these contrasting sources and approaches since both make sense. However performers choose to make sense of these measures, it is worth considering each version's pros and cons.

Notes

1 Joseph Kerman et al. "Beethoven, Ludwig van." *Grove Music Online,* www.grovemusic.com (accessed 11 June 2012).

2 The Letters of Beethoven, Vol. I, ed. and trans. Emily Anderson, quoted by William S. Newman in *Beethoven on Beethoven: Playing His Piano Music His Way* (New York: W. W. Norton, 1991), p. 54.

3 ibid., p. 54.

4 William S. Newman in *Beethoven on Beethoven: Playing His Piano Music His Way* (New York: W. W. Norton, 1991), p. 46.

5 ibid., p. 32.

6 Rosenblum, P. Sandra. *Performance Practices in Classic Piano Music* (Bloomington: Indiana University Press, 1991), p. 60.

7 ibid., p. 87

8 ibid., p. 87

9 ibid., p. 229

For Further Reading

Beethoven-Haus Bonn. http://www.beethoven-haus-bonn.de/sixcms/detail.php?template=portal_en (accessed 11 June 2012).

Drake, Kenneth. *The Beethoven Sonatas and the Creative Experience.* Bloomington: Indiana University Press, 2000.

Joseph Kerman, et al. "Beethoven, Ludwig van." *Grove Music Online. Oxford Music Online.* http://www.oxfordmusiconline.com/subscriber/article/grove/music/40026 (accessed 11 June 2012).

Newman, S. William. *Beethoven on Beethoven: Playing His Music His Way.* New York: W. W. Norton, 1991.

Rosenblum, P. Sandra. *Performance Practices in Classic Piano Music.* Bloomington: Indiana University Press, 1991.

Schindler, Anton Felix. *Beethoven As I Knew Him.* ed. Donald W. MacArdle. trans. Constance S. Jolly. Mineola: Dover Publications, Inc., 1996.

Schlosser, Johann Aloys. *Beethoven: The First Biography.* ed. Barry Cooper. trans. Reinhard G. Pauly. Portland: Amadeus Press, 1996.

Sonneck, O. G, ed. Beethoven: Impressions by his Contemporaries. New York: Dover Publications, 1967.

Audio Credits

Patrych Sound Studios, New York

Six Variations

on a Swiss Song

(22) VAR. II
26
30
VAR. III
(33) Minore
sempre piano e legato
37
41

VAR. IV

(44) **Maggiore**

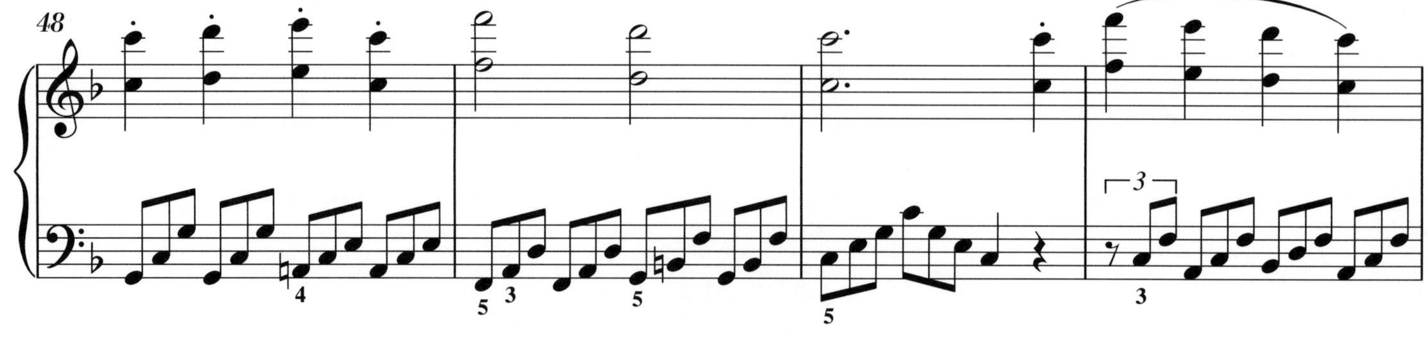

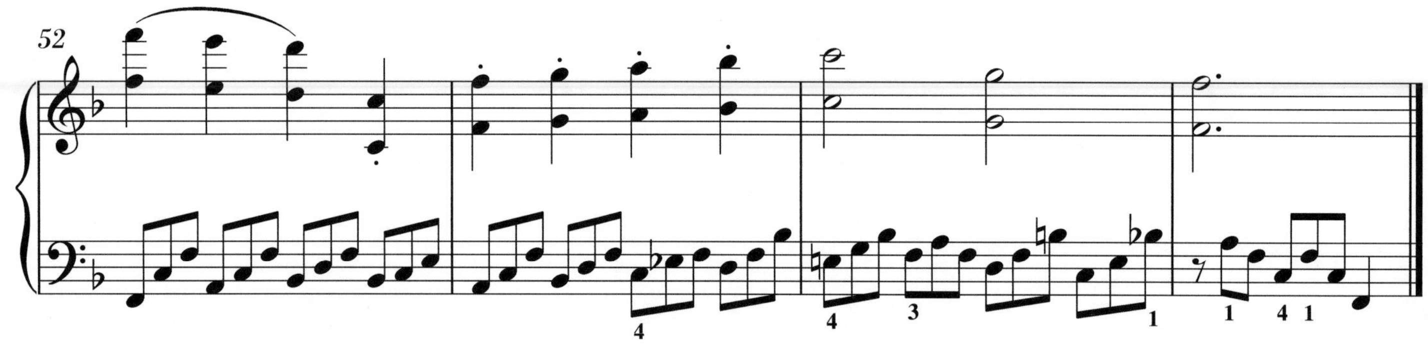

(55) VAR. V

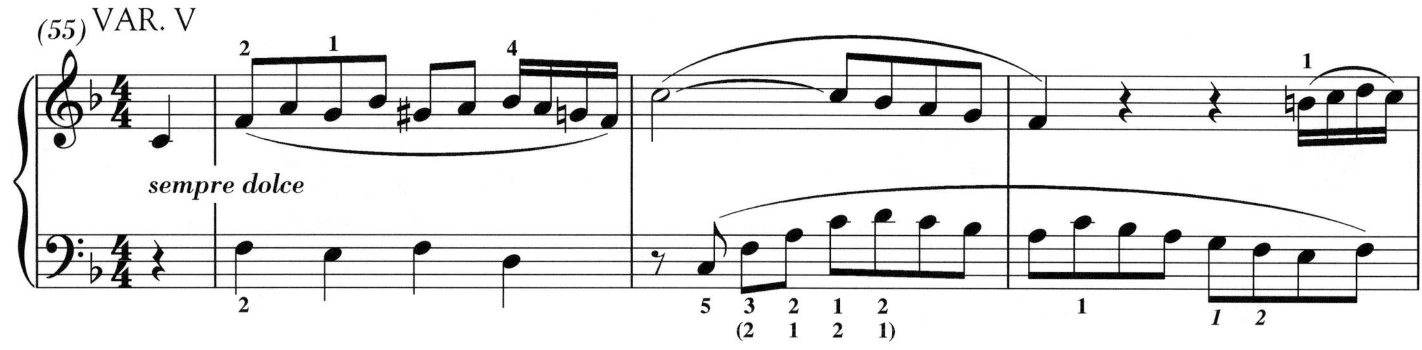

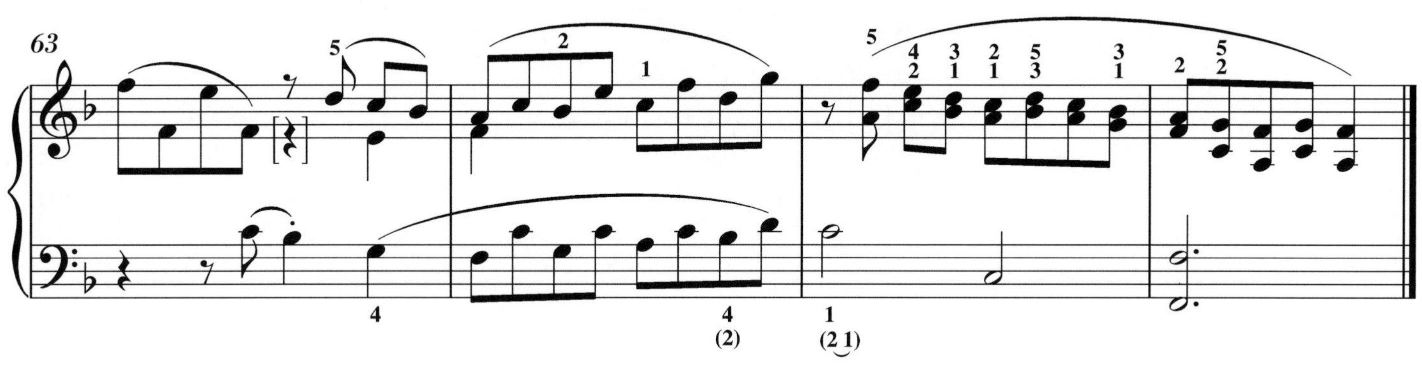
63

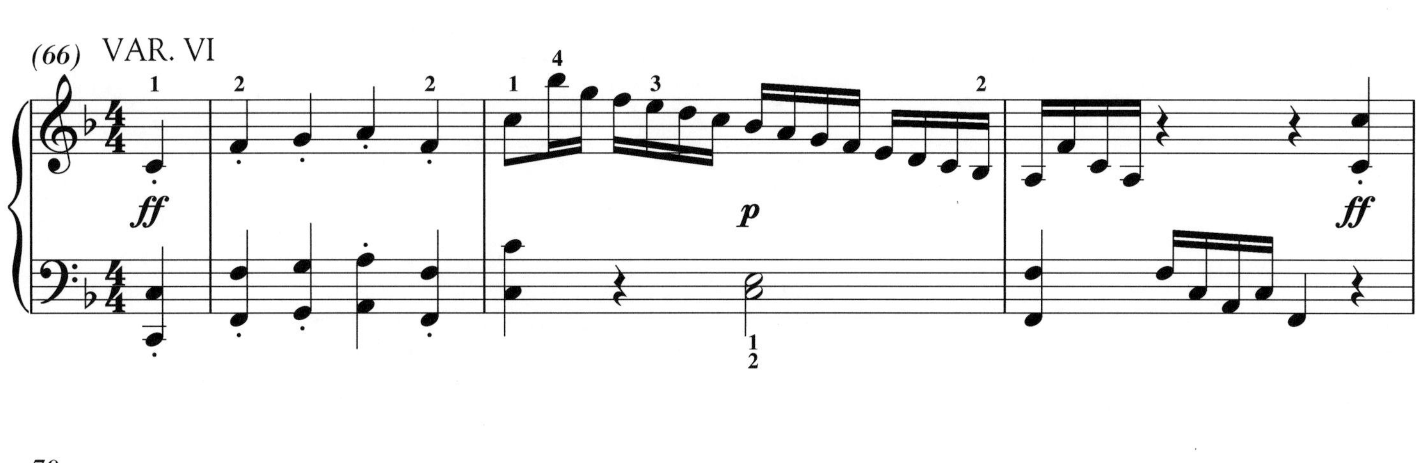
(66)
VAR. VI
ff
p
ff

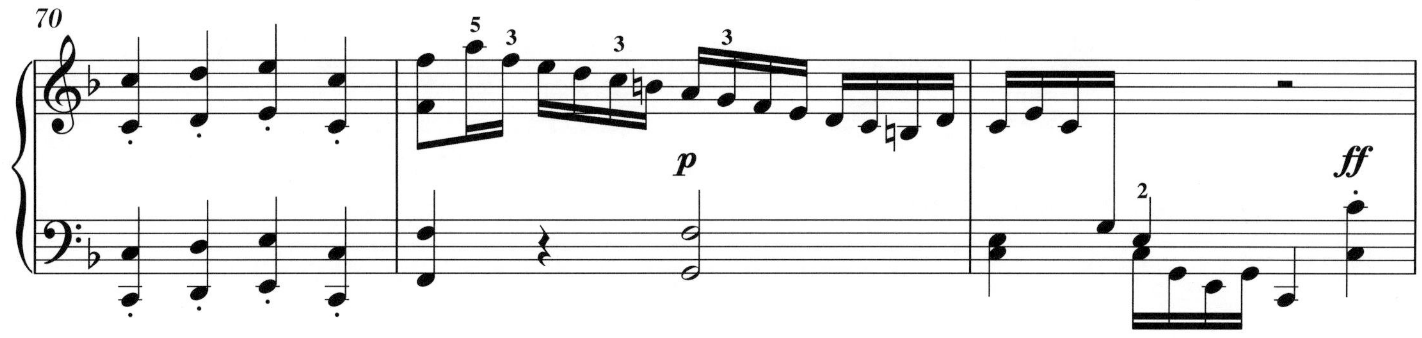
70
p
ff

73
tr
tr

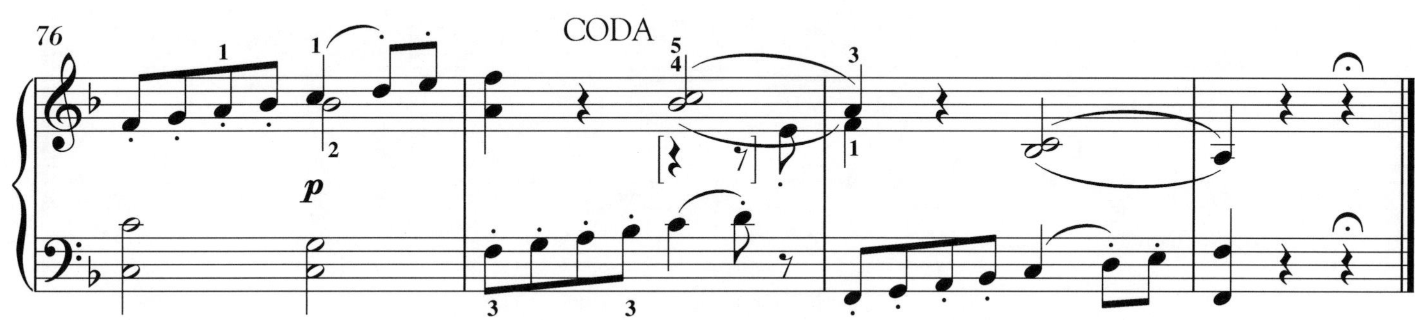
76
CODA
p

Dedicated to Count Karl von Lichnowsky

Nine Variations

on "Quant' è più bello"
from *La Molinara* by Giovanni Paisiello

Ludwig van Beethoven
WoO 69

THEME
Allegretto

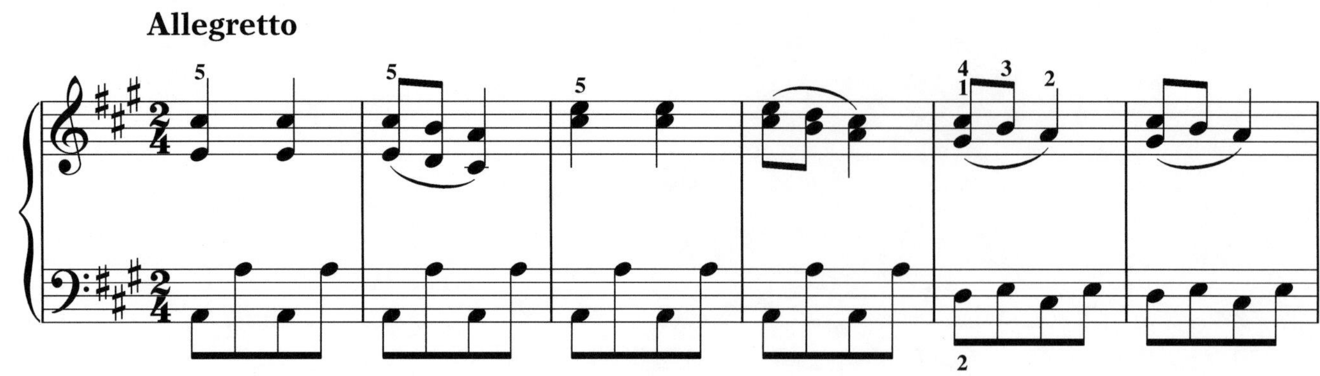

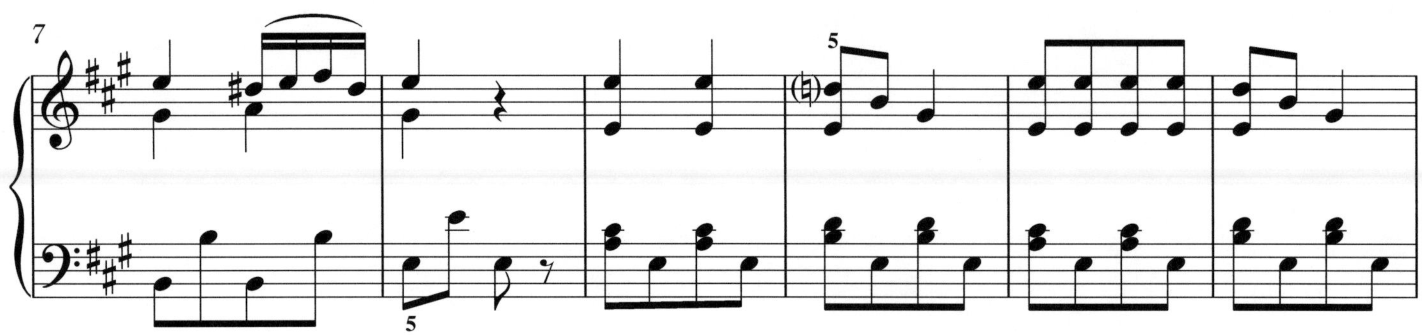

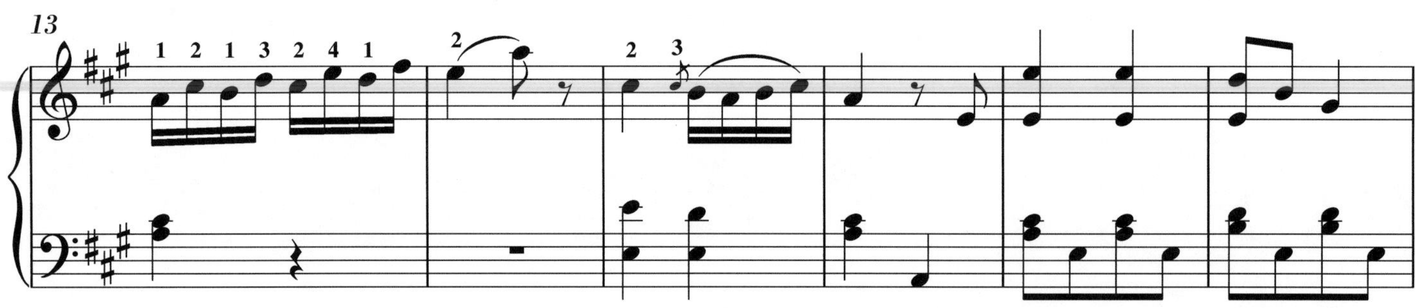

(24) VAR. I
29
34
39
44
sf
sf
sf
sf

(48) VAR. II

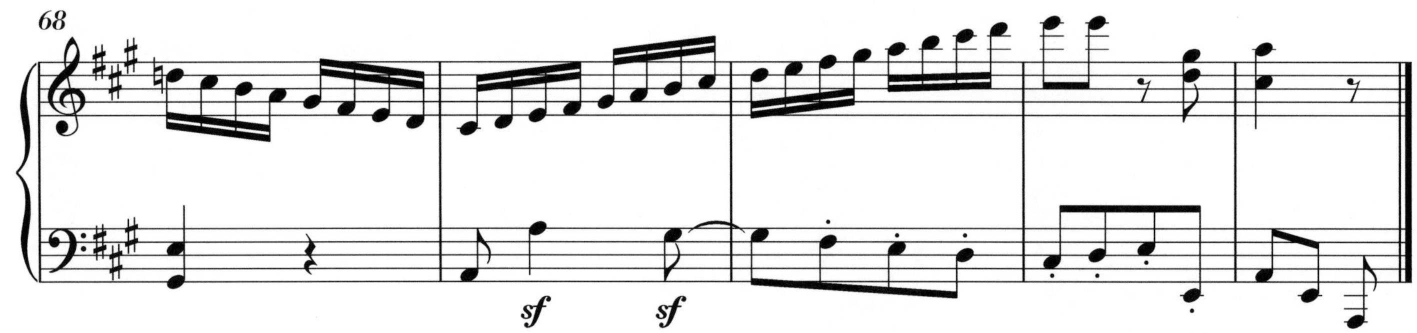

(72) VAR. III

77

81

85

89

93

VAR. IV

VAR. V
Maggiore
(120)
pp
125
130
135
sf
sf
140

VAR. VI

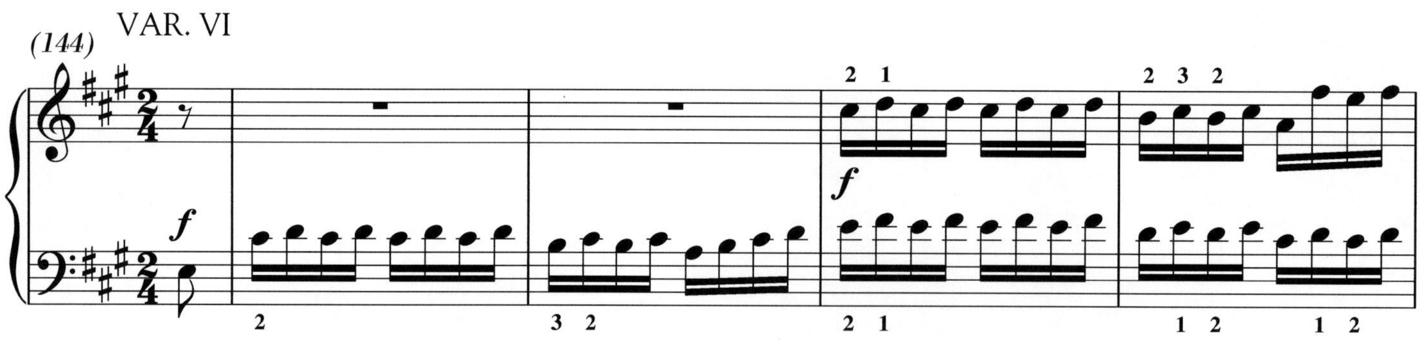

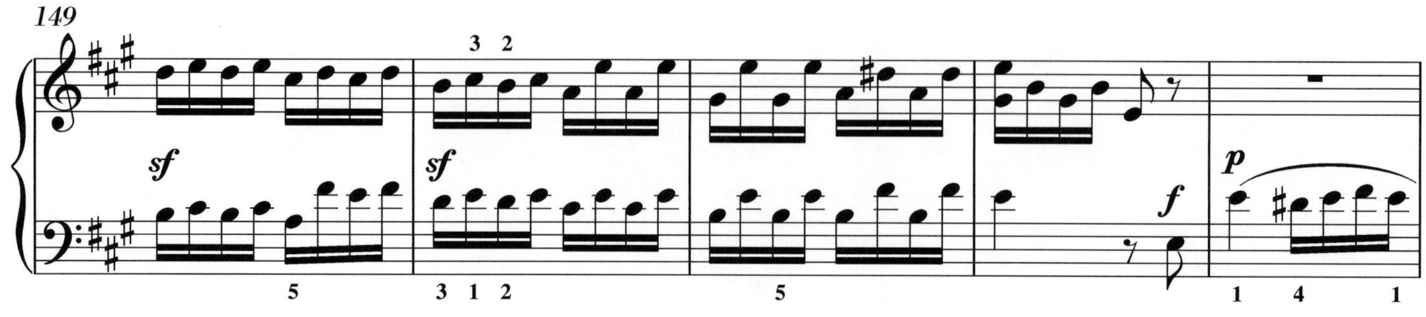

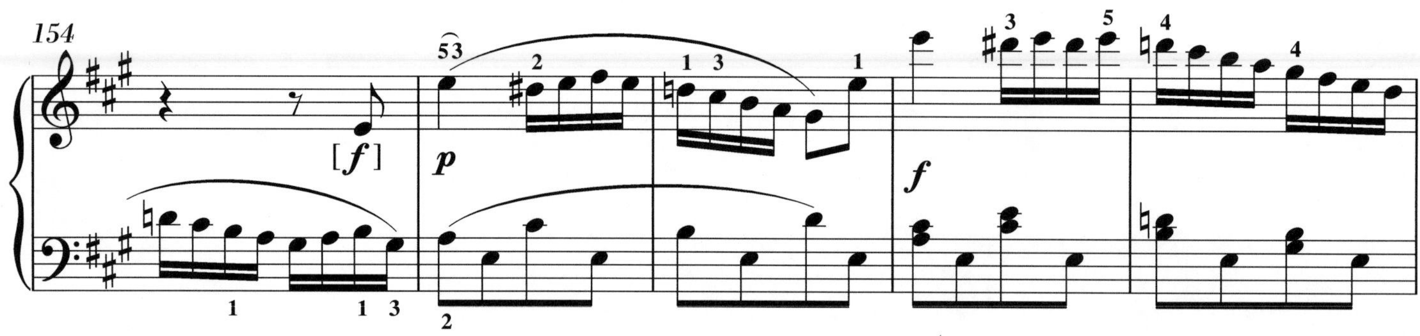

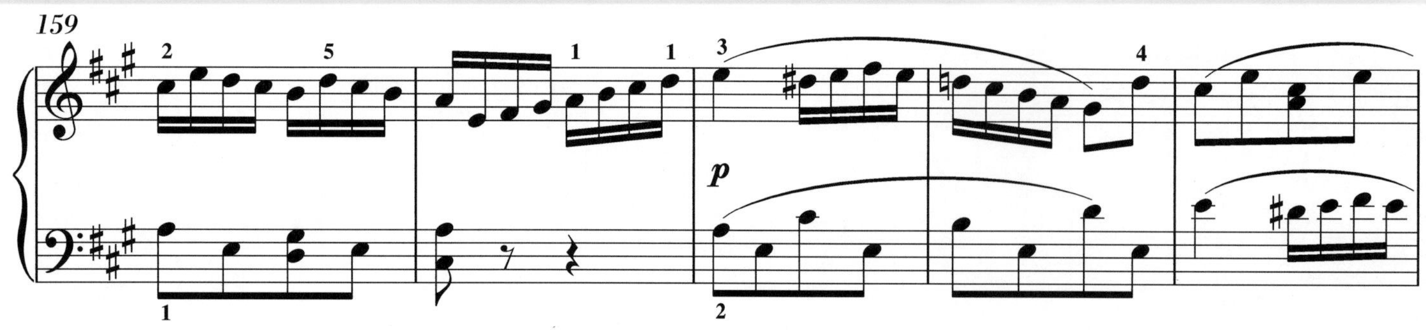

(168) VAR. VII
p
173
sf
178
sf
183
sf
sf
188

VAR. VIII

(192)

196

200

sf *sf*

205

209

sf *sf*

213

VAR. IX

Tempo di Menuetto

238
241
p
244
247
pp
250
p

253
pp
pp
f
256
259
sf
sf
262
sf
sf
265
p
pp

Six Variations

on "Nel cor più non mi sento"
from *La Molinara* by Giovanni Paisiello

Ludwig van Beethoven
WoO 70

23
26
29
32
35
38
sf

(40) VAR. II
43
46
49
52
55

58
(60) VAR. III
65
69
73
77
sf

VAR. IV
(80)
85
89
93
fp
97
(100) VAR. V

(120) VAR. VI

[m.g.]

144
[m.g.]
148
152
156
sf
160
164

Eight Variations

on "Une fièvre brûlante" from *Richard Cœur de Lion*
by André Ernest Modeste Grétry

Ludwig van Beethoven
WoO 72

VAR. II

(64)

69

73

85
89
93
VAR. III
(96)
101

105
sf
sf
5
108
1
1
1
1
5
143
4
111
5
(4)
5
2
1
115
4
1
3
4
118
5
2
1
sf
121
sf
sf
sf
5
2
1
4
2
sf
4

125

VAR. IV

(128) **Minore**

136

141

147

154

VAR. V
(160) Maggiore
cresc.
165
(tr)
f
p
sf
170
sf
174
sf
179
sf
sf

184
cresc.
188
f
p
VAR. VI
(192)
f
p
197
200
f
p

205
208
f
p
212
ff
p
216
f
p
p
221
cresc.
ff
VAR. VII
(224)
p

229

234

239

244

248

252

VAR. VIII

(256) **Allegro**

p

cresc.

263

269

p

275

cresc.

279

f

284

288
p
295
tr
301
tr
f
307
312
316
ff

321
CODA
pp legato
pp legato
325
329
334
cresc.
Presto
339
f

343
347
p
351
cresc.
ff
p
cresc.
355
ff
359
f
f
f

Six Easy Variations
in G Major

Ludwig van Beethoven
WoO 77

THEME
Andante, quasi Allegretto

(24)
28
(32) VAR. II
sf
35
38

(40)
sf
sf
sf
43
cresc.
sf
46
f
VAR. III
(48)
ten.
p
52
ten.

(56)
60
ten.
ten.
ten.
64
68
ten.
ten.
VAR. IV
(72)
Minore
p
76
tr
tr
(12)

(80)
84
tr
cresc.
decresc.
pp
VAR. V
Maggiore
(88)
91
94
1.
2.

(96)
99
cresc.
102
1.
2.
VAR. VI
(104)
107

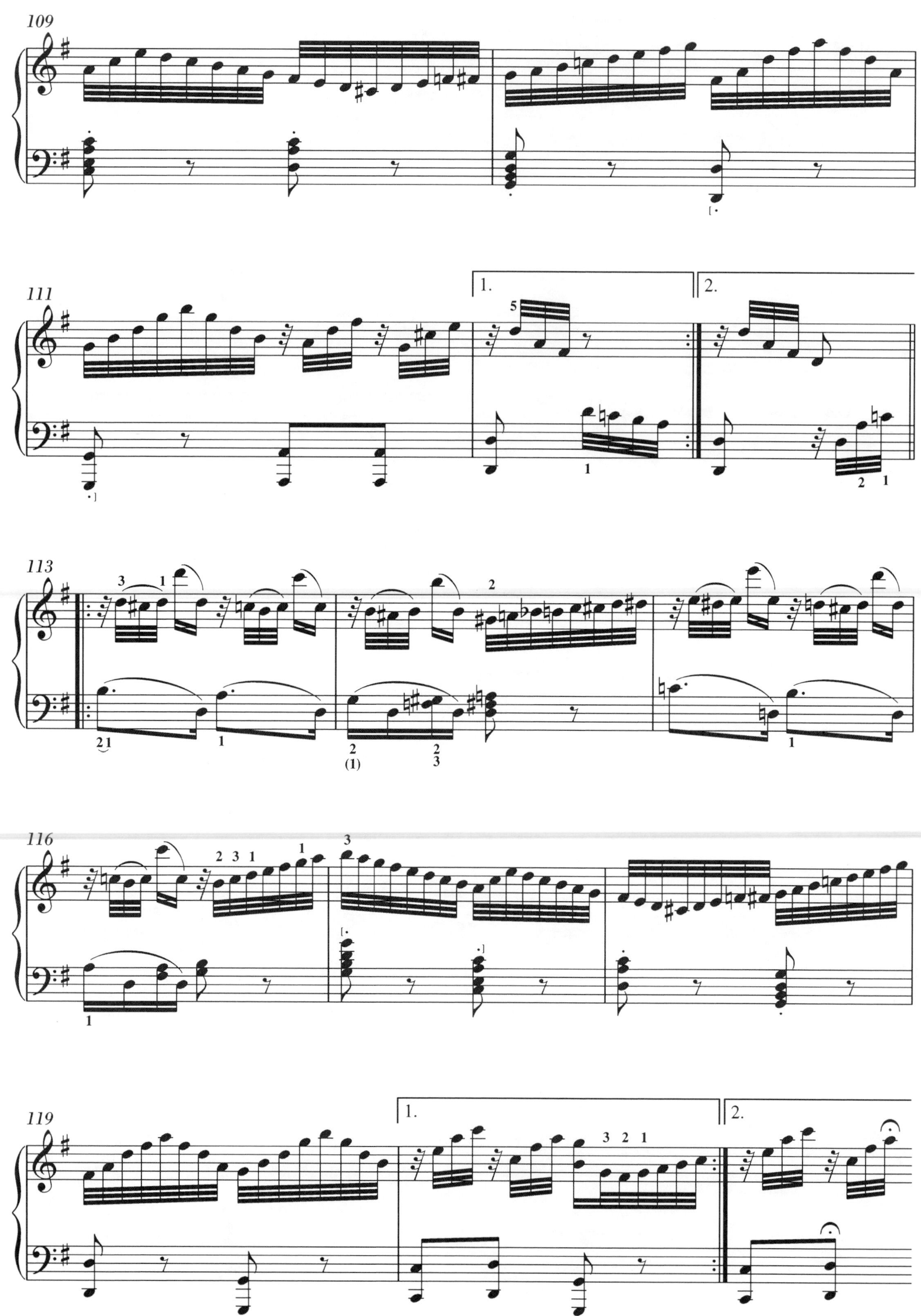
109
111
1.
2.
113
116
119
1.
2.

CODA
(121)
124
127
130
133
cresc.
ff

ABOUT THE EDITOR

Immanuela Gruenberg

Active as a recitalist, chamber pianist, teacher and clinician, Immanuela Gruenberg has appeared in the United States, South America, Israel, and the Far East. She has presented workshops, master classes and lectures on piano performance, piano literature and pedagogy. Critics have praised her playing as "supreme artistry" (*Richmond News Leader*), "lyrical and dramatic" (*Buenos Aires Herald*) and noted her "delicate sonorities" (*Haaretz*, Israel). She was lauded for her "highly intelligent" writing, "scholarly" and "well thought out" research, for lectures that "exceeded our highest expectations," for programs of "unusual interest" and for having "spoke[n] intelligently about each piece" (*The Washington Post*).

She began her musical career in Israel, performing as soloist and as member of the Tel Aviv Trio in venues that include the Chamber Music Series of the Israel Philharmonic Orchestra, the Israel Museum in Jerusalem and the Tel Aviv Museum of Art. She appeared on Buenos Aires Classical Radio, and recorded for Israel's Classical Radio where she was featured repeatedly. In the United States she appeared on stages such as the Kennedy Center for the Performing Arts, the Corcoran Gallery, the Strathmore Mansion and the Smithsonian's "Piano 300" series, celebrating the 300th anniversary of the invention of the piano. Other "anniversary" performances include lecture recitals in Israel and the United States on Schubert's posthumously-published sonatas—the topic of her doctoral dissertation—in honor of the composer's bicentennial anniversary and a performance of Josef Tal's Concerto for Piano and Electronics in honor of the composer's 85th birthday. She presented lectures and clinics at colleges and universities, for various MTA chapters, at conventions, at the World Piano Pedagogy Conference, as well as for the general public. Dr. Gruenberg taught master classes at the Central Conservatory of Music in Beijing, China, the Liszt Academy in Buenos Aires, for the Latin American Association of Pianists and Pedagogue, and in various venues in the US and Israel. A much sought after adjudicator, Immanuela Gruenberg also served as chair of the Washington International Competition. She currently serves on the editorial committee of American Music Teacher, the official publication of Music Teachers National Association, on the National Conference on Keyboard Pedagogy's Committee on Independent Music Teachers, and is Vice President for Programs for Montgomery County, MD, MTA.

A magna cum laude graduate of the Rubin Academy of Music of the Tel Aviv University and a thirteen-time winner of the America Israel Cultural Foundation scholarships, Dr. Gruenberg is the recipient of numerous prizes and awards. As a scholarship student at the Manhattan School of Music she completed the Doctor of Musical Arts program in only two years. She studied piano with Arie Vardi (for over ten years) and Constance Keene and chamber music with Boris Berman and Rami Shevelov. She also coached with Pnina Salzman and Thomas Schumacher.

A teacher of award winning students, Dr. Gruenberg was a teaching assistant at the Manhattan School of Music in New York, a faculty member of the Music Teachers' College in Tel Aviv and the Levine School of Music in Washington, DC, and maintains an independent studio in Potomac, Maryland.